SIGNPOSTS FOR LIVING

A PSYCHOLOGICAL MANUAL FOR BEING

DR KIRSTEN HUNTER

BOOK 1
**CONTROL YOUR CONSCIOUSNESS –
IN THE DRIVER'S SEAT**

BOOK 2
UNDERSTANDING MYSELF – BE AN EXPERT

BOOK 3
**MINDFULNESS AND STATE OF FLOW –
LIVING WITH PURPOSE AND PASSION**

BOOK 4
**UNDERSTANDING OTHERS –
LOVED ONES TO TRICKY ONES**

BOOK 5
PARENTING – LOVE, PRIDE, APPRENTICESHIP

BOOK 6
NAILING BEING AN ADULT – HAVE THE SKILLS

A MEANINGFUL LIFE

DEVOTE YOURSELF TO:

1. **KNOWING** YOURSELF,

2. **LOVING** OTHERS,

3. **LOVING** YOUR COMMUNITY,

4. **GRATITUDE** FOR THE MOMENT, AND

5. **CREATING SOMETHING** THAT GIVES YOU MEANING AND PURPOSE.

First published 2021 by Kirsten Hunter

Produced by Indie Experts P/L, Australasia
indieexperts.com.au

Copyright © Kirsten Hunter 2021

The moral right of the author to be identified as the author of this work has been asserted.

Except for the purposes of reviewing, no part of this publication may be reproduced or transmitted in any form or by any means, electronic or mechanical, including photocopying, recording or any information storage or retrieval system, without the written permission of the author. Infringers of copyright render themselves viable for prosecution.

Cover design and image by Zach Lawry @ Mates Rates Screen Printing & Design
Edited by Jane Smith @ www.janesmitheditor.com
Internal design by Indie Experts
Typeset in URW DIN by Post Pre-press Group, Brisbane

ISBN 978-1-922742-08-7 (paperback)
ISBN 978-1-922742-09-4 (epub)

Disclaimer: Any information in the book is purely the opinion of the author based on personal experience and should not be taken as business or legal advice. All material is provided for educational purposes only. We recommend to always seek the advice of a qualified professional before making any decision regarding personal and business needs.

To Jon

PREFACE TO THE SERIES

This series of books is actually a conversation that I have had with thousands of people over the last twenty years of clinical psychology work. From approximately 42,000 hours of conversations with clients of all shapes and sizes and from all walks of life, all struggling during their various stages in life, I have learnt so much. When you have the same conversation that many times and you see progress, you see where the value lies. I want to share this conversation with you.

'Signpost for Living' is written out of sheer frustration and exhilaration in equal measure. I have limited hours with my clients. This series of books is the information, across the breadth of 'being human' areas, that I would cover with clients if there was no limit to time. This is my 'ideal situation' series, to share with others how to understand and master ourselves. We are pretty dodgy at being human. We really have very little clue about how we work – we don't fully understand our emotions, our behaviour, our neurology, our physiology – or how to live with purpose, calmness, contentment and joy, with our loved ones and within ourselves. This series covers all of these life-challenge hotspots and things we need to learn about ourselves. If we get support, encouragement, and general guidance in these areas, we can get on track quickly. Life can expand and boom us into more contentment and happiness.

How amazing life is if we allow it to be.

If you get a new puppy, it is wise to put in the time to train it; you can enjoy your pup so much more once it's trained. Your pup becomes easy and fun to walk, reliable on your carpets, and an enjoyable character. This is strangely true for *us* too. By studying our thinking, emotions, behaviour and styles of relating to others – really getting a solid level of self-awareness and having a robust skillset – we can enjoy ourselves and our world so much more. And no, we do *not* need to be puppies to learn new tricks; we can learn as adults, at any stage of life. No excuses here. It is absolutely, profoundly, exasperatingly ridiculous that we do not all learn this information routinely at school. 'How to be human, class 101'. Humans have the code to develop physically, but we need more information to develop psychologically into full adults. Not learning these basic life skills can leave us feeling insecure, disconnected and unsafe.

Life is growth. Life is a work in progress.

This is what these books are about. We do not know everything about 'being human' – far from it – but we do know a fair bit. This knowledge, which comes largely through the profession of psychology, is not, however, common knowledge. And yet it should be. It needs to be. We need a manual for being human, for without it we are driving blind.

This series is based on clinical evidence and sound reasoning. It provides clear, calm direction – not all the answers, but solid signposts. Time to share this knowledge with everyone.

WHAT TO EXPECT IN THE 'SIGNPOSTS FOR LIVING' SERIES

The books in the 'Signposts for Living' series are independent but complementary; by strengthening and cultivating one area you enhance all of the other areas simultaneously. There is not much point fixing one hole in the boat when the other holes are not receiving attention. This is not a piecemeal series. We need to cover the whole of human functioning. In this series there will be chapters you need, chapters you don't, chapters that talk to you now, chapters that will tap you on the shoulder in your future. The 'Signposts for Living' series is written for everyone: all ages, mums and dads, grandparents, young adults and teenagers finding their way.

The books are broken down to first explore (in Book 1) how controlling your consciousness can help you grab the reins to your nervous system, thoughts and emotions. Relevant side-alleys that are common traps to dodgy thinking are included. We then flesh out your personal issues in Book 2: *Understanding Myself*. The importance of being awake in life and aware of your present moment is celebrated in Book 3, along with the gem of living with purpose and passion in a state of flow. 'Signposts for Living' then broadens in Book 4 to discuss understanding our relationships with our people (the good, the bad and the ugly). The true complexity of parenting is then dissected in Book 5. Finally, the art of nailing being an adult is fleshed out in Book 6, revealing the excitement of reaping the rewards of becoming a thriving mature human.

To make the books as concise and user-friendly as possible, I have avoided references, footnotes and other scholarly tools as much as possible. The goal is for you to be able to access and use this valuable information without feeling bogged down or needing to have specialised, background knowledge. To acknowledge my sources and guide you to delve deeper, if you wish to, I have included 'further reading' lists where relevant at the end of each book.

Welcome to understanding your humanness.

BOOK 5
PARENTING – LOVE, PRIDE, APPRENTICESHIP

CONTENTS

INTRODUCTION	TO THIS BOOK	1
CHAPTER 1	GOOD ENOUGH PARENTING	5
CHAPTER 2	APPRENTICESHIP MODE	7
CHAPTER 3	TAKING IT PERSONALLY	9
CHAPTER 4	CRITICISM	11
CHAPTER 5	LEARNING HOPE	12
CHAPTER 6	LET DAD BE PRIMARY PARENT TOO	14
CHAPTER 7	LECTURING	16
CHAPTER 8	NEGATIVE LANGUAGE	18
CHAPTER 9	YELLING AS A WARNING HORN ONLY	20
CHAPTER 10	AUTHORITARIAN, AUTHORITATIVE, PERMISSIVE: WHICH ARE YOU?	23
CHAPTER 11	PRIDE AND LOVE, NOT JUST LOVE	28
CHAPTER 12	OPPOSITIONAL BEHAVIOUR ... HELP ME!	30
CHAPTER 13	SPECIALISED PARENTING SKILLS	37
CHAPTER 14	NEVER, NEVER, *NEVER* SAY SOMETHING THAT YOU CANNOT CARRY THROUGH ON AND CONTROL	54
CHAPTER 15	TIME TOGETHER	56
CHAPTER 16	THEIR FRIENDS ARE CRUCIAL	57
CHAPTER 17	TEENS NEED TO FEEL LISTENED TO	59
CHAPTER 18	DON'T COMPARE KIDS	61
CHAPTER 19	KIDS WHO SAY THEY ARE FAT	62

CHAPTER 20	FAMILY AND SIBLING CULTURE OF LOVE	66
CHAPTER 21	CHANGING GEARS: PARENTING TEENAGERS	68
CHAPTER 22	FLOW IN THE FAMILY	70
CHAPTER 23	TECHNOLOGY = KID IN A CANDY STORE; RESTRICT THE CANDY	72
CHAPTER 24	SLEEP PLEASE	75
CHAPTER 25	KIDS THRIVING THROUGH PARENTAL SEPARATION	79
CHAPTER 26	TEENS BECOME CAVE DWELLERS	82
CHAPTER 27	MONEY MANAGEMENT SKILLS	84
CHAPTER 28	SIGNIFICANT CLINICAL CONDITIONS: IF IN DOUBT, GET HELP	86
CHAPTER 29	SCHOOL IS LIKE A ZOO	87
CHAPTER 30	TEENAGERS WHO VOTE US OUT	89
IN CONCLUSION		91
FURTHER READING		93
ACKNOWLEDGEMENTS		94
ABOUT THE AUTHOR		96

INTRODUCTION TO THIS BOOK

I have been asked by clients consistently over the last twenty years to write a parenting book. Here it is. It's an ambitious idea, and there is a huge amount to cover.

You do not need to be a perfect parent; you need to be a 'good enough' parent, but this is still a pretty high bar. I've worked with adults, teens and children, and I enjoy all of the work because I need variety and challenge to stay fresh. I especially enjoy my child work, however, because it is so profoundly meaningful to help set a child up to be on a strong footing for the rest of their lives. To address a problem area so that it actually becomes a strength for them rather than a painful anchor point is wonderful beyond words.

I am always amused by the inevitable question by new clients: 'Do you have kids?' Despite my qualifications and experience, this is where I get my credibility. I pass this test when I say yes, then with more questioning, I explain that I have five boys. At the time of this writing, Lachlan is twenty-one, James is eighteen, Tobias is sixteen, Jack is nine, and George is seven. With this I'm 'in'; my trustworthy quotient goes up. I understand this. Parenting is one of those things you can only comprehend from the inside, the marathon that it is, with profound joy, meaning, frustration, and fear all wrapped up together.

Parenting is perhaps the role in which we need to be the most mindful; we are the nurturer, the leader and the protector, so it is essential that we are reflective and purposeful in our parenting. Strange, then, that so many parents yell at their children, and when at breaking point, say things they regret, and know will harm their children. Many parents hit their kids. This is truly damaging, as the primary lesson that hitting teaches is fear and violence. We end up with kids who become increasingly fearful in their response to the world and who reach for hitting as their coping mechanism. They learn to copy their parents. Then they get angry at them for hitting others!

As role models we can easily become their number one cause of harm. It's like the manager, leader or coach becoming the bully. Our parenting role is a massive responsibility. Someone who is good at 'adulting' is miles ahead in terms of being set up for good parenting. All the topics in this series, while primarily aimed at development of the *individual*, can also apply to setting us up to be thriving parents. It is an amazing thing to feel on track and confident in our parenting. It is, however, soul destroying to look back and know that we have not nurtured enough and have actually done harm. Let's grow our children with care and strength. I am happy to say there is bucket loads of common sense here, but we need to be able to step away and get some distance to see this. That is what this book can help us do.

Just a quick note: I do not want to create parental guilt here. I would argue that parental guilt is perhaps one of our strongest emotions. It dangerously has us going in circles, berating ourselves and making the situation worse. I am all about parental *action*. If it's broken, fix it; don't just sit in a puddle feeling sorry for yourself. We can even get things more on track with our adult children. The key is insight and ownership. By learning our patterns, owning them and communicating them to our children, we can repair or rebuild bridges in our relationships with our kids. Nothing can be strengthened and repaired until we have been able to identify and address the damage. Ignoring the harm and just plastering it over may look okay on the surface, but the trust and deeper connection is blocked. It can become a superficial relationship, which is not our goal, and remains a reminder of our true needs not being met. We remain in a state of neglect with the people who we actually wish were our rock and our closest and strongest advocates.

Let's look at the health of our parenting relationship. We will look more closely at these issues when we untangle oppositional defiant disorder in a moment, but here is an overview to orient us. Let's go straight to the heart of it. We cannot parent with negative emotions, with any revenge in our heart when we are feeling hurt, or with emotional withdrawing from our children (the infamous silent treatment). We cannot emotionally guilt them or emotionally intimidate them and we cannot take their child and teenage antics personally. This means no yelling, no emotional venting and no extended lecturing when we are worked up. When our munchkin is misbehaving we have to separate them from their behaviour. It is bad behaviour and poor choices, it is not that we have a bad child, so please never, never, *never* say 'bad girl' or 'bad boy'. This is worse than calling them names or criticising them. This is you saying that their person – their core – is bad. If you wanted to shred their self-esteem, this is how you would do it.

Our goal is to provide a stable, nurturing family environment. This means not being reactive during the hard times. We want them to feel safe to come to us during the tough, vulnerable and humiliating chapters in life. Why would they if we have previously become emotionally reactive when we have been disappointed by their behaviour? Plenty of parents have told me 'My kids can talk to me about anything.' They are speaking about their ideal. Then their kids tell me in session, 'No way. Mum or Dad would crack it at me, they're the last person I'd talk to.'

Yes, we need to be superhuman. When we are the parents, we are the backbone of our family, we are the leaders. We need high standards for ourselves and we need to earn the honour of being their role models. We need to behave congruently and avoid being hypocrites, as they will sense fraud a mile off and then feel contempt for us.

CHAPTER 1
GOOD ENOUGH PARENTING

On some level, we have all felt the wound of being let down in one way or another by our parents throughout our early years. Even in the best-case scenario and even with super loving parents, our parents cannot always be available for all of our needs, and we are going to have different opinions from them. This is called '**good enough parenting**'. Which means being attuned and supportive parents who are *human* – parents who miss the mark on occasion, and miss cues regarding their children's needs.

This 'good enough parenting', as it turns out, is actually the optimal type of parenting, as it teaches children that although their cup is fairly full, the world is not *always* going to respond to them the way they want. This prepares children for the real world, which is far from consistently and sensitively responsive. It also helps children to learn 'frustration tolerance' – that is, they learn to tolerate and self-soothe when their needs have been frustrated. From this they can learn the skill of patience.

So relax, parents; you do not need to be perfect. Far from it. We need to be sensitive, responsive but still fallible humans. Children need to gently learn that their needs are not always met and they are not the centre of the universe.

CHAPTER 2
APPRENTICESHIP MODE

Childhood and teenagehood are really apprenticeships for adulthood. We are growing our young to become optimal adults, so that they are as independently capable, grounded in confidence and as interpersonally skilled as possible. This of course then sets them up in good stead for life. We want them to be in a strong position to enter the world and to find contentment, meaning and happiness. To do this, we need to expect from our children and teenagers increasing skills of mindfulness of others and a high level of contribution in the home. If they are physically and cognitively capable, then they should be on their way to achieving those life skills. Otherwise you are doing their apprenticeship for adulthood for them.

Imagine if you were doing an apprenticeship as a carpenter, and the boss was picking up your tools and doing all the work for you. Come the end of your apprenticeship, you would not be skilled, you would not be capable, and you most certainly would have no reason for confidence in your profession. It is exactly the same for us learning to 'adult'. Childhood and teenagehood are the years of apprenticeship, and we parents need to keep an eye on the horizon of adult life skills needed as we gently and gradually ask more of our growing child. Hundreds of parents have said to me 'It's just easier if I do it.' There is no wisdom here, just a knee-jerk quick fix. It's time to think of the big picture and who you are really helping in the long term.

When a child goes to school, they go to learn; they do not have the knowledge to begin with. It is a process of not knowing, then learning, practising, then knowing. So too with our child's behaviour and emotional and interpersonal skills. We are their teacher, we are their role model, their nurturer. Of course, as their role model, we need to deserve the role. We need to be 'value adding' to their lives, and not be a liability for them. More than anything, we teach them how to behave through *our* behaviour. A lot of parents are furiously frustrated that their child or teenager is misbehaving, when, in truth, this just means that they are yet to learn a better form of behaviour – and it is actually *the parent's* job to teach them, shape them and guide them. We strangely expect children and teenagers to have it together and behave. Yes, that's the goal, but you are on the journey with them. So let's slow it down, break it down and figure it out together.

CHAPTER 3
TAKING IT PERSONALLY

You as the parent create the parameters of the choices available to your child or teenager and you help them make good decisions. If they haven't started making these good decisions yet, that's okay; persevere with providing limits, incentives, consequences to help them decide. Your job is to nudge them in the right direction. But don't take it personally. That's like a teacher expecting her students to know all of the classwork and then taking it personally when they don't. This period is literally a learning phase, an apprenticeship for adulthood. They are guaranteed to get a lot wrong, to misbehave and test the boundaries. That is what childhood is. If you want a perfect child, one whose behaviour will give you nothing to complain about, then you need a non-human child, perhaps a robot.

When we become emotionally involved in parenting and we take their misbehaviour personally, we confuse the issue for the child, and we distract from what we are trying to teach them. This is because the focus becomes about the tension between you and your child, rather than their problem behaviour. Guaranteed, your child will come away from the interaction *not* focusing on their problem behaviour (which *should* be their sole focus), but upset with you and with a heightened emotion about the conflict.

CHAPTER 4
CRITICISM

What if we kept track of the percentage of our interactions with our children that consist of demands and criticism? Sadly, this can be a massive majority. How do we as humans respond to being told what to do when it is done in a demanding, short-fused way? We are likely to resist. With this comes resentment, which then progresses to an obstinate tone. We refuse or respond with a passive-aggressive 'I forgot'. The situation deteriorates from there. Does this sound familiar? Common child and teen defiant responses, perhaps?

Does criticism of others actually work in changing their behaviour, in parenting effectively? No. Yet we continue to do it. Why? Because we are using the interaction to vent our frustration. We are kidding ourselves if we think that we are parenting when we are criticising or using a demanding tone with our child.

CHAPTER 5
LEARNING HOPE

What is our primary task as parents? Beyond day-to-day emotional, physical and functional well-being, it is to teach them that we can have hope and happiness in our imperfect world.

It is only through example that we can instil these life skills – by *doing*, not just saying and expecting. The reverse is also true. It is important that through our role modelling we do not instil our fears in our children. Too often, sadly, this is exactly what we do: we transmit our uncertainty, fear of failure and anxiety onto our child. Anxiety is contagious. Our children sense anxiety in us and they are actively shaped by it; it happens even before our toddler child is verbal. If our children approach something difficult, they can sense our hesitation and lack of belief of a positive outcome. If we walk into a crowd, they can sense our fear of the crowd. Another classic example is the hysteria about stranger danger. Yes, we do need to skill our kids up, but we need to keep it in perspective. The risk of a car accident is exponentially higher than the chance of a child abduction. But where do we place our emphasis in child education? The areas that produce intense fear in us parents. We do not emphasise safe driving enough in schools, but instead drum in stranger danger. This does not statistically make any sense.

Another example of the negative role modelling that our children absorb and foster is our pessimism towards our world and our future. It is profoundly sad to encounter a pessimistic young person. At the age that they should be curious, feeling invincible and enthusiastically launching themselves into life, they actually feel hopeless and helpless. In my experience, most of these children have caught this contagion from their parent's outlook and relationship with life. We need to instil in our children a positive belief in finding a way through and working towards the horizon. Let our sense of hope shape our child's world view, not our personal anxieties.

CHAPTER 6
LET DAD BE PRIMARY PARENT TOO

Don't rescue fathers. Usually, but by no means always, when it comes to babies and toddlers, mums are front and centre, and dads are a bit on the sideline. Of course there are all sorts of dynamics between parents, in same-sex relationships and hetero relationships. This is too much of an observed pattern in hetero couples, however, for me not to make special mention here. Nevertheless, whatever your gender or relationship dynamic within your home, if the shoe fits, apply this wisdom to yourself.

In general, mums know the routine, know the tricks of the trade, and dads come in and assist mums. What this means is that dads often report not feeling confident with their young child's daily processes. They can feel awkward and like outsiders when the child is left in their care for short periods, and mums complain that everything is on their shoulders.

Here is the thing: it is wonderful if the dads can have some time to work it out for themselves and become fully involved so that they can build confidence. You need to go through the messy period of chaos to get there. They need time to experiment, to master their parenting skills, and to have a sense of ownership over their fathering role. It is important that they take the reins for a while, and regularly, so that they don't just feel like they are in helper mode, or even visitor mode. It is okay for fathers to do things differently, to do things *their* way. As long as there is communication about parenting practices that are really crucial to the child – such as safety and health issues – we need to embrace that we are different people with different approaches.

It is so important that dads have some time to be the primary parent without the mum around, so that they can find their feet and work it out their way. Then both parties can be confident and capable parents, and they can both have the children interchangeably. The punchline: mums need to step away and go out for the day regularly, and dads need to step up and break through the anxiety of being a solo pilot so they can find their feet and become confident. How wonderful for everyone: Mum gets a break and can be fresh for everyone, and the little person and Dad have some precious one-on-one time.

CHAPTER 7
LECTURING

We should really call lecturing 'venting' because if we are honest, that is what it is. We justify our lecturing by telling ourselves that we are educating our child – that we are explaining why they should not do what they are doing. But in truth, if you were calm, if you were not triggered by their misbehaviour, then you would not want to lecture them. We lecture because our buttons are being pressed, we are taking the misbehaviour personally and we are too close to the situation. We are releasing our exacerbation and desperation onto our child. Lecturing happens when we are wanting to pressure them into submission, and we are trying to impose our power.

Do we actually think that the child does not know what they are doing is wrong? Even if our child could benefit from some learning and direction, do we as humans learn when we are being treated with cranky and repetitive criticism? Do we learn with raised voices attacking us? Absolutely not. Actually, we put our walls up in defence and we shut our ears. The reality is that if we want our children to learn something new about their behaviour and our family expectations, this has to be done in a safe space, with a calm and positive, collaborative tone. These conversations are great; they are about building and enabling everyone to feel part of the solution.

So, in summary, lecturing is a disaster. If you lecture, quit the habit. This will be very hard to do, which shows you even more how it is actually about your emotional reactivity and your need to vent. Confronting, but true.

CHAPTER 8
NEGATIVE LANGUAGE

Okay, here is a big one. As discussed in previous books in this series, it is vital that we use *positive* statements, not negatives, to explain what we want. Try not to use double negative statements with your children and teenagers. If you read 'Don't touch the wet paint', what does this lead you to think? The answer is that you start thinking about touching the wet paint. You hadn't had this thought until you read the sign. An example of the contrast between positive language and negative is saying, 'Speak to each other with kindness', instead of, 'Don't speak to each other rudely'.

We might feel comfortable using the negative or double negative statements, and uncomfortable with positive directive statements. But positive statements build, educate and explain what we *do* want, not what we *don't*, while negative statements are damaging and sabotaging. Just as we should not use double negative statements in our general communication and our self-talk, we should not use them with our children. When a brain receives a negative statement, it pays attention to the negative statement first, it fuels it, then works to move away from it. When a positive statement is used, it reinforces the positive statement. Simple. Let's use our neurology for our benefit, rather than having it work against us.

CHAPTER 9
YELLING AS A WARNING HORN ONLY

I'm walking from a café with two girlfriends, and we have seven kids with us. Across the road is the park. In an instant, the children race towards the park, mindlessly about to cross the busy road. The other two mothers and I all in unison yell 'STOP!' My three kids stop, frozen; the other four keep running, with their mothers in fast pursuit.

I don't intend this as a brag, although it absolutely sounds like one, and I am sorry for that. It is a beautiful illustration of what we should reserve yelling for. To the other two mothers' shock, my three stopped in their tracks because they are not at all familiar with me yelling. I don't yell. Literally. Yelling does not happen in our house. I have been trained in the power of keeping a low, quiet voice to maintain authority. My friends continue to be shocked as they explain that they yell at their kids all the time.

Don't lose your poker face.

When we raise our voice in any naggy or yelly way, we have given away our power. We sound and are desperate. If you lose your 'poker face' in parenting, you have just given your children the upper hand.

Yelling need only be used as a warning bark from the parent to the young. Keep it for dangerous situations in which you want your kids to listen and respond with urgency. Don't desensitise your kids to yelling. If you do, you will lose it as an extremely valuable tool. This is apart from the fact that yelling in the home takes away your power, makes a home unpleasant to live in, makes relationships punishing and just gives your children negative experiences and feelings. It actually makes poor behaviour worse. Staying calm and using even tones requires emotional regulation, confidence and the use of other effective techniques, which I'll explain further below.

Just to be clear: when you speak to your kids, turn off their technology and speak to them in a quiet, purposeful and private voice. When I come home, whatever I need to sort with each of the kids, I come up to them individually and we have an intimate conversation. If there are others in the room, I stand one metre away and we have a quiet word. I do not humiliate them by letting the rest of the family know their business. If the child turns their head away from you or puts their hands over their ears, ignore that behaviour and speak as normal anyway. They can hear you, and although they might not want to listen, they *are* listening. But of course they won't acknowledge your words. You do not want to get involved in a tug-of-war over this for no reason.

The key is that yelling is not effective for parenting; it just dissolves the power of your voice. Keep a raised voice for those rare, perilous occasions so that you can lasso your children out of danger.

CHAPTER 10
AUTHORITARIAN, AUTHORITATIVE, PERMISSIVE: WHICH ARE YOU?

You may be familiar with the three different parental regimes. These parenting styles are on a spectrum, and it helps to acknowledge where you currently sit on the spectrum.

AUTHORITARIAN PARENTING	AUTHORITATIVE PARENTING	PERMISSIVE PARENTING
Sergeant Major	Approachable reasonable leader	Fearful friend

Authoritative is the parenting model that is healthiest and most balanced. It involves giving clear guidance and boundaries as a parent. The communication style is open, but the child knows that the parents expect certain standards of them.

Authoritarian parenting is a dictatorial style of parenting. Authoritarian parents impose their will and are very harsh. (Think: 'You're under my roof, you do it my way'.) The children are not allowed to have their vote on child- and teen-based decisions; they do not have a voice. Individuality is not allowed to flourish.

Permissive parenting involves deferring parental decisions to the child. Rather than being the clear leader, the parent is the friend. The child does not have boundaries or direction from the parent. The family works as a fairly democratic collective. The parent fears that the child will be upset with them if they parent, and therefore accommodates the child's demands. The parent is missing the important point that *they* are an adult with adult skills and knowledge, and that their child is a *child* – a cub – unaware of what they don't know and ill-equipped to survive in the adult world.

Have you thought about which parenting style your parents used with you as a child, and which one you use as a parent? If you have a partner, what parenting style does he or she demonstrate? Are you replicating or protesting your parents' parenting style? If our parents were authoritative, we commonly replicate and take the lead from their approach. If our parents were authoritarian, then it is common for us to parent in a knee-jerk opposite way, and we can be very permissive for fear of being like our parents. A less obvious pattern emerges when our parents raised us in a permissive way, but a safe bet is that we will be permissive in our parenting. Of course, there is no direct prediction – and we can decide our own approach – but there are definitely patterns.

Authoritative parenting is the most sound approach because it is important that while the child needs to grow up feeling loved and respected, it is essential for parents to establish limits. These limits are necessary because we want our children to be the healthiest and most mindful versions of themselves.

With authoritarian parenting there is an obsessive need for control on the parent's part. They are often anxious about the child's future, and manage that anxiety with control. This routinely leads to debilitating and destructive power struggles within families, as the child and teenager are developmentally needing to experiment with and voice their emerging individuality. This drains the happiness from the family and leads to resentment on both sides, and often passive-aggressive resistance from the child. The child cannot stand up to the parent; it is not safe, and they are not empowered. The parent will be forceful with their control if the child has a different opinion or is not subservient. What the child *can* do is not get on board with the parent's request, and passively protest. They can develop an understandably defiant mindset. In survival mode, the kids become clever in hiding their actions, all the while fearful and angry that they have to be so cunning to be their own individual. Kids of authoritarian parents often leave the nest, only to fall down. They have not had the personal freedom to experiment with being a young adult and making their own choices. They have a poor capacity to internalise limits as they have only experienced overpowering external limits. They leave home ill-equipped for independent choice, control and accountability.

With permissive parenting, the risk is overindulgence, resulting in a spoilt child or a child who has no regard for boundaries in society. They have not gone through the process of direction and accountability, and often go on to make impulsive, poor choices or not to understand that standards are expected of them in society. These young adults can find it hard to work and exist comfortably amongst others. They may have a poor work ethic because everything has been handed to them; they have been overindulged. They may have a poor level of self-awareness and accountability because they have not had boundaries and have never needed to be mindful of their actions. There is a high risk that they will have learnt to be entitled. In their future relationships they may not understand that life is about finding a 'win:win' solution, that life doesn't always go according to their terms. They often dominate their partners and tantrum or sulk when they don't get their own way.

Authoritative parenting, on the other hand, is a bit like raising bear cubs: when times are good, and when there is scope for the child to explore and experiment, then exploration is embraced and encouraged. There is freedom to grow. The cubs are encouraged to adventure independently and extend themselves. When a behaviour is dangerous to the child's personal development, to their interpersonal relations or their need to take responsibility as a family member, however, then Mum and Dad bear pull them into line. The child feels safe, knowing that there are limits, and they respect their parent/s as a result. They like being in the watchful and proactive care of their assertive parent. But they can grow and learn and explore their own individuality under the watchful eye of their parent.

The aim of a parent is to have their children admire and respect them, not to like them. When there is respect and admiration (and fairness), the child will enjoy their parent. The authoritative parent is taking the 'wise' path, not the 'popularity-seeking' (permissive) path or the 'power-hungry' (authoritarian) path.

CHAPTER 11
PRIDE AND LOVE, NOT JUST LOVE

We love our child, yes. We tell them we love them. That is great. But just as important as telling them that we love them is telling them that we are *proud* of them and *why* we are proud of them.

Our children develop their self-concept and their positive self-talk largely from the verbal feedback that parents give them. Yet we are not great at this. I am not talking about the gushing parent who thinks their child is perfect and the best at everything. There is no reality here, and the child will grow up out of touch with themselves, the world and others. I am talking about praising effort, personal investment, areas of genuine strength (strengths of character, strengths of value system), personal highlights, personal accomplishments.

> A self-imploding basis for confidence.

Notice that I did not include praise for their looks. Our child's *substance* needs the celebration, not their 'wrapping'. Our looks have no substance, no depth of meaning. If our self-talk and confidence is based on our looks, then we are in deep trouble, for when our 'packaging' (our looks) alters with time, we can feel as if we are losing ourselves – when in truth we have just not learnt to look within, to look deeper. Our self-validation needs to come from within, from ourselves – not from other people, or from worrying about what other people think of our appearance. Don't set your child up for this shallow, profoundly vulnerable, and inevitably self-imploding basis for confidence.

Our job is to hold up a mirror to our child and let them know that we see them – their unique person – and celebrate them. Infants start with a blank canvas of self-talk; we have the honoured role of helping them to become acquainted with who they are and helping them to discover and feel confident in themselves. Take this creation of their self-talk template very seriously. We care about nourishing them physically; this is nourishing them psychologically.

CHAPTER 12
OPPOSITIONAL BEHAVIOUR ... HELP ME!

Every child has oppositional moments. They are flexing their muscles, trying to get their way, testing you out, or just tired and beyond reason. When a child is routinely *extreme* in paying no heed to the parent's direction and has frequent meltdowns and aggressive behaviour, they may meet criteria for **oppositional defiant disorder**.

In truth, this is only a description of behaviour *while it is relevant*. It is a diagnosis that only applies while the problems remain. Once the child has been managed well by switched-on, specialised parenting and they are kept on track, then the diagnosis is no longer valid. It is not a long-term diagnosis; it is only used when it is current. Oppositional defiant disorder has been made a diagnosis because 1) these oppositional behaviours can become extremely severe and hijack any form of family harmony, and 2) the diagnosis allows professionals to communicate about the problem, study it, and work out best practice in how to intervene.

The great news is that whether you have the typical parenting challenges, or if you have a full-blown oppositional child, the same parenting skills apply. You also need to use these advanced parenting skills with *all* of your kids in unison, not just your more tricky kid. This is optimal parenting for all, and fairness all around. The difference is just that with an oppositional child, it is *essential* to learn and use these parenting skills; you have no choice if you want a good outcome. With a non-oppositional child, on the other hand, you can sometimes get by with just 'shoot-from-the-hip' parenting. But there is no doubt: all families will benefit from understanding what makes children tick and understanding basic child psychology. This means informed parenting – how refreshing!

So here is the breakdown. The majority of kids are very influenced by external forces; they want to please, they want to fit in, they want to comply. We call these kids **'negatively oriented'**, as they are primarily motivated to *avoid negative outcomes*. They want to keep their parent and their teachers happy with them. They want to find out what is expected of them so that they can follow this path set out for them and not be distressed by disapproval or conflict. This is the typical child; you just have to look disappointed and it will have an impact and shape their behaviour.

Then there is the child whose motivation is mostly influenced by internal forces. This is called **internal motivation**. They don't necessarily *seek* to step off the path from everyone else, but they themselves have to choose the path. They are motivated by their own personal carrots. They have to decide that they themselves agree to behave a certain way – that the behaviour is in line with their personal motivation. They dance to their own beat. Enter the personality of the oppositional child.

We call them '**positively oriented**' because they are primarily motivated by their own *personal positive outcome*. As an example, a negatively oriented child will do their maths homework so that their teacher does not disapprove of them and they don't stand out (unless they love maths, in which case they would be doing it for pleasure). In contrast, a positively oriented kid will do their homework *only* if they like maths or they themselves have decided that they want to stay in their teacher's good books. Unlike the negatively oriented child, who is inclined to want *all* the teachers to have a good opinion of them, the positively oriented child casts their vote on each of the teachers individually. They may choose to behave well for all of their teachers, or only for their select favourites. The contrasts between external and internal motivation, and punishment avoidance and reward as motivators are striking.

Disappointed looks, reactive emotional parenting and punishments pulled out left, right and centre, *do not work* with oppositional children and teenagers. Actually, this reactive parenting can often make their behaviour worse. Our only choice is to work with their motivational model.

We need to figure them out and then take their world view into account as we work with them. They do not want us to figure them out, because they don't want us to be able to shape their behaviour. *They* want to have the upper hand.

Actually, these personalities routinely resent being parented. They think being a child is restricting and insulting. They want the power and the choice in their lives. Yet while they may *want* the full freedom of choice, they actually become stressed when given this responsibility and freedom. For example, imagine a child demanding to be in the driver's seat of a car – once they're driving they'll become panicked and overwhelmed. Ironically, if an oppositional child is given freedom to parent themselves, they misbehave much more. This is to wake the parents up and push them to step in and parent – to put in boundaries and move the child back to the passenger role. The child wants and needs to feel contained and safe again through your proactive parenting. Here we have the conscious child pushing for control, but the subconscious child pushing to be parented. Confusing ...

I have met and worked with many hundreds of these internally driven kids. I really enjoy them. One reason that I am half decent in this clinical area is that I was one of these positively oriented kids myself. Actually, my school experience is the best example that I have come across of positively oriented behaviour, and when I share it with client parents, they nod with relief as they can relate to the themes. Let me share.

As a kid, I liked peace. I liked to cruise along, so I was rarely in trouble. This is because it was my priority to have peace, not because I feared getting in trouble. I was a very independent kid, very much in my own world with my own agenda. When I went to high school, I distinctly remember at the age of thirteen working out how this whole high school system worked here in Australia. Basically, I knew that I wanted to go to university. I had grown up through financial hardship and I wanted financial security, and I knew I would need to find something to keep my mind challenged. I then discovered that only my grades from senior year would be relevant for entry into university. Great! I was sorted.

I had a plan: for the next four years I would enjoy school socially, enjoy sport, but not care about grades. I would learn enough so that I had the foundational knowledge for senior year, and I would submit all my assessments so that I didn't have the inconvenience of getting into trouble, but that was it. And I did just that. I went on to pass or fail each subject through these years with no care or regard. I did not care that the teachers did not think or know that I was a bright kid. I was unfazed about people around me doing well; I did not compare myself and I did not feel threatened, because I had a plan. In my mind, all of the assessments over these four years were not going to help me; they would just end up in the bin. My poor mother was so frustrated, but while I did not like this, it was not a motivator for me. Come senior year, I literally told my friends that I wouldn't hang out with them until the holidays, and I put my head down and got the grades. I strategically got the grades to get me into university. Job done. During my earlier years the incorrigible side of me enjoyed seeing some of the teachers dismissing me as not capable and not academic. I knew my final chess move was yet to come. And then when I started to excel, I really enjoyed the annoyed response of those teachers who had been dismissive of me. *I had the control, not them, and I wanted them to learn not to dismiss kids.* I was a classic positively oriented kid. I sailed towards my own horizon and in my own way. It is just fortunate that I was motivated towards a good horizon.

While the typical kid who is negatively oriented is a breeze to parent, the positively oriented kids have many strengths also. Positively oriented kids prescribe less to society's expectations; therefore they are largely protected from problems like anxiety and depression, which are based on insecurities arising from comparing ourselves to others. This is an enormous theme for many with anxiety and depression. Also, positively oriented people are more likely to think and dream outside of the box. This can make them inspiring leaders and creators in our world. The key is for them to find inspiration for positive and grounded goals in the future.

It is a really interesting exercise to reflect on what kind of kid you were. As parents, our orientation is very relevant. Parents who were positively oriented will be able to relate to their kids who are positively oriented, while parents who were negatively oriented as kids will just find their positively oriented kids' behaviour to be bizarre and illogical. By the way, this motivational orientation continues in adulthood, but becomes less clear as our personalities become more complex and we become increasingly shaped by life experience.

CHAPTER 13
SPECIALISED PARENTING SKILLS

Here we go. Children look to their parents to ensure their needs are met. The fuel for children, their 'currency', is the *parent time* and the *parent emotion*. This is not conscious; this is on a subconscious level. Here is the clincher: they will take this time and emotion in any form that it comes – positive time and emotion, or negative time and emotion. Fuel is fuel. On a conscious level the child will prefer positive time and emotion, of course. But on a subconscious level, they will take it in any form they can get it. If it means that the way to get the parent's time and emotion is through negative behaviour, therefore earning them negative time and emotion, they will take it.

It is argued that this is a survival response. Let's think about prehistoric times. Little Johnny has had a quick smile from the parent and a nice 'good job' pat on the head, and he then goes off to play alone. Little Albert is acting up, getting yelled at by Mum and Dad. Which child is going to survive when the sabre-toothed tiger comes prowling? By being actively engaged with Mum and Dad, little Albert has proximity with his parents; they are plugged in with him. They're giving him negative time and emotion, but they are involved. Little Albert will therefore be protected from danger, while little Johnny is alone and defenceless.

> Child currency = parent emotion + parent time.

It all sounds a bit strange, but it is this simple: children are programmed to get emotion and time from their parents, and they often figure out that they get more of it from misbehaving than behaving. Think about it: when our kids do something we like, we say 'that's great', 'good job'. Our emotion is about a 2/10, and our time investment is brief. When we are upset at our child's misbehaviour, however, we are more likely to react with emotion. We will easily hit a 6/10 – even an 8/10 – in intensity, and we are prone to lecture and vent at them, which leads to extended time invested in the child. Well done, team! Our child may look upset (and feel it at a conscious level), but we have just fuelled them up with our time and our emotion, and taught them on a subconscious level that that worked well. Better keep misbehaving in the future.

Parents say to me all the time, 'But I give my child lots of my (positive) time.' This can be true, but it is irrelevant when you realise that kids don't have a quota to fill. They will never have enough; they just want more and more of the parent's time, and the parent's intensity of emotion and time is much more if they misbehave than if they behave well. This is their internal programming. Checkmate to the child.

Just to confuse things further, when our children behave positively, our responses can be very predictable. Our kids can almost script our predictable, positive words and tone. 'Good job, Harry', 'Thanks for that, Emma'. They know which things we will praise them for. We think we are doing a great job by praising our kids, but we are far from potent here. Our praise fades into predictability. In contrast, when our children misbehave, our response varies enormously. We may try to stay calm, or we may just let ourselves yell. Our reaction would depend on whether it is the second misbehaviour or the tenth. Our response would depend on whether we feel pressured, or are rushing out the door, have guests, are on the phone, have sick children, or have other misbehaving children ... the list goes on and on and on! We are also very unpredictable regarding which consequence we choose to pull out of the hat. We keep trying different punishments. Our punishments also change enormously based on the previous list of changing variables. So, basically, with negative behaviour we are unpredictable as parents.

This unpredictability in parenting is called **intermittent reinforcement** and it is the most powerful way to reinforce human behaviour. This is the foundation of gambling. If we sat at a poker machine and continually received five cents every round, we would quickly get bored and stop. But we can sit there getting mostly nothing interspersed with the occasional dollar and be thinking, *What's going to happen and when?* and we can become hooked. This is intermittent reinforcement. So basically, commonsense reactive parenting has us reinforcing our children to misbehave. Great!

Here is another twist: remember the negatively oriented kids? They are motivated to avoid negative responses. So, the enormous reinforcement effect of negative attention and negative emotion is largely crossed out by the fact that these kids want to avoid negative interactions. They cancel each other out. The positively oriented kids, by contrast, do not find the negative interactions and negative emotions to be something they are particularly keen to avoid. They can therefore tolerate the negative tone, and they can just line up and take the fuel that is coming their way: their parent's (negative) time and emotion. This is why we can actually be making our oppositional kids worse with our heightened, cranky, emotional reactions and our time-extended lecturing. Does this make sense?

So, what do we do to parent our positively oriented kids who are potentially oppositional? We reverse our commonsense parenting. When our child is behaving well, this is when we reinforce their behaviour by giving them our time and our emotion. When our child is behaving poorly, we starve them of our time and our emotion. When it comes to consequences, we need to make them clearly stated and predictable; we need to make them **deterrents**, not **punishments**. What is the difference?

There is an enormous difference. A punishment is usually erratic; it changes. A deterrent is clear and pre-stated, and it discourages us from behaving a particular way. For example, the police have deterrents for speeding. We know if we get caught we will lose our driving points and we will have to pay a penalty fee. We know this and we don't want this, so we think twice about speeding. If the police changed their consequences randomly – sometimes making no consequence, sometimes a talking to, sometimes demerit points, sometimes a penalty fee – then we might roll the dice. We would gamble and hope to get out of a consequence. We would not be as motivated to not speed. This is the same with kids. If the consequence changes, the kids do not have a clear and predictable consequence in their minds to act as a deterrent. With parenting, punishments are usually inconsistent, while deterrents are locked in, consistent and predictable.

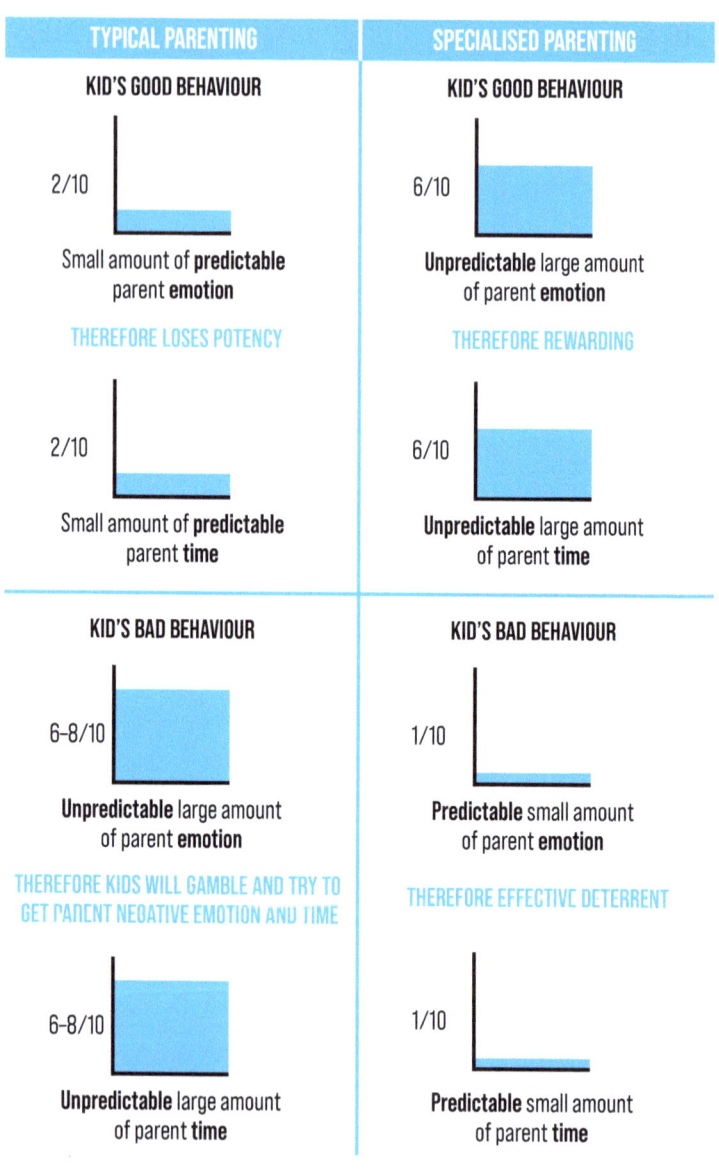

So, let's put this together:

PARENTING POSITIVE BEHAVIOUR

There are four ways to reinforce behaviour: time, emotion, affection and token rewards. Let's look at them.

1. The fuel of our **time**. 'I love that you just brought your lunchbox from your bag, how about I come play Lego with you for a bit?' You can delay this if needed: 'Dale, I love that you just made your bed. I'm just going to hang out this washing and then I'm going to come and play with you. You pick what we are going to do.' It is likely that Dale is going to behave well until his parent comes to spend time with him. This time with your child needs to be in *their* world; park yourself and enter their interest area. Sitting on the floor with a child is a good start. Humour their interest for five minutes. And yes, the child will then not want to go – they rarely have enough of parent one-to-one time – but when they know it will come around again soonish, they can tolerate you leaving more easily. If they tantrum when you go to leave, then this is bad behaviour and you respond as outlined below. This reinforcement approach is profoundly powerful to the child. It is only five minutes of your time, so take a child-centred break from your adult world.

2. The fuel of our **emotion**. Try to hit a 6/10 in intensity of positive emotion used. If you are embarrassing yourself, you are on track. Your kids will probably at first look shocked at your degree of positive emotion, then

they will think you are being ridiculous, but they will love it. Subconsciously they will *really* love it. Their sponge will be filling up quickly.

3. The fuel of our **affection**. A hug, a warm hand on the shoulder, a kiss. Children need affection; again, it fuels them up.

4. You can throw in **token rewards**. But the essential key is that they do not know what they are getting or when. It is a surprise; therefore, it is powerful. And the key to this is that you be *unpredictable*, so that they don't know *which* behaviours you will reinforce, *when* you will reinforce them, or *how* (with time, emotion, affection or rewards). Keep them guessing. Spin a wheel in your head. Which of their behaviours will you reinforce, and which way will you reinforce? Remember, you are primarily giving them your time and emotion for their positive behaviour in an unpredictable way. *You* hold the cards here. This is the intermittent reinforcement. The potent poker machine of parenting.

PARENTING NEGATIVE BEHAVIOUR

The procedure
1. *All* parenting parties (including the highly involved grandparents) need to be *consistent in their expectations* of their children. If you are not consistent then you are being confusing and intermittent in your response.

Also, the parent with the lower standards is likely to get the worse behaviour when the kid/s are in their care. Sit down as parents, work it out, trade off what is important to you, compromise. This is essential.

2. Have a positive family meeting and explain to the kids what the expectations are. Explain the below plan to them: that they will get involved parents when they behave well, and this planned parenting response when they behave poorly. It is crucial that you go through a role play where you show them the steps if they make poor behaviour choices. Perhaps use a teddy or even a parent as the 'child who makes poor choices'. For example, 'Imagine Teddy (or Daddy) keeps kicking the ball in the house. This is what is going to happen.' And run the process through step by step so the child becomes the expert. Let the child take that authority role as Teddy (or Daddy) is being parented. Kids love playing the teacher role. This family meeting is about being fair and transparent. They need to know the information so that they make an informed decision that it is in their best interests to behave well (once they have tested you out many, many times to see that you mean it and will be consistent and not cave in).

3. Follow this planned parenting response:
    a. <u>First</u>. **Give instructions** to do something (for example, wash dishes), or to stop doing a poor behaviour (like bouncing a ball inside the house).

b. <u>Second</u>. If they have not done what you have asked, then you follow with a **warning with brief words:** 'I've asked you to play with the ball outside, not inside. This is your warning'. Or 'I've asked you to do the washing up; do it now, please. This is your warning'. You do not need to mention the consequence. They already know from what you have set out that the consequence will follow. We don't want to get into the trap of lecturing, and we don't want to always be coming across as negative and threatening.

c. <u>Third</u>. If they do not listen to this warning, then you need to apply the **consequences** (I will explain consequence in a moment).

There is an exception to this stepped approach when your child does *harm*. When it comes to doing harm, we want to give a strong message that it is not tolerated, and we do not want to give them a chance to continue to inflict harm. So if a child does harm in saying something cruel to another, being physically violent to another (sibling, parent, animal), or breaking or damaging an object, then you move directly to the consequence. There is no warning if a child does harm; consequence comes immediately.

The consequences
Time Out

The consequence for young children of under approximately nine or ten is to go to '**Time Out**'. There are clear rules about Time Out.

We ideally use a room that is *safe* and *boring*. Many use the toilet if it is a separate room with no sink (take out all flushable items), or a spare, boring room. Try not to use their bedroom if you can help it; it is not ideal because it is stimulating. Time Out duration is one minute per year of age, so for a seven-year-old it is seven minutes, and for a ten-year-old it is ten minutes. Use a timer, and let them know you are using it. The duration is between them and their timer, not you. This is fair and transparent. This time starts from when they are quiet. So while they are complaining, yelling out or tantruming, the time does not start. It starts when they are quiet. This is for the sake of teaching them emotional regulation. They need to learn to calm themselves down. It becomes their priority to calm themselves down to start the Time Out and get it over with, rather than choosing to whip up a storm. They learn that tantrums don't work. Great lesson. Also, if we let them out of Time Out while they are tantruming, this would directly reinforce this behaviour.

When you take them to Time Out you make a very simple statement of what they have done wrong and then you say, 'Now it's time for Time Out'. A simple statement might be 'You hit your brother', 'You didn't unstack the dishwasher', 'You kept playing with the ball inside'. Then again you say, 'Now it's time for Time Out'. You are very simply explaining the problem behaviour and their consequences – that's it. No more talking, no conversation, no explaining. You are mute. You are not giving your time or emotion. When you state this, you are being firm and calm, even bored.

Your emotion is 1/10. Your child gets nothing out of their parent. You take them by the hand and guide them to Time Out. Although of course you are often feeling a lot of emotion, annoyance, anger, or desperation, you must be poker-faced; never show them your emotion. Don't let them know that they have pressed your buttons; don't give them that power or that dump of negative emotion.

By the way, a switched-on child will try to control Time Out. They might say 'I like Time Out', or 'I'm going to stay in Time Out'. These are all games. Just say, 'No problem' and ignore this diversion technique. Enjoy their ingenuity.

Withdrawal of privileges
After this age (ten years and up, approximately), we use **withdrawal of privileges**. For most kids this means taking away access to technology. It is important that you break this down into small chunks of time so that you have many chunks of time to work with, and to make it fair to the child. It is essential that the child understands that the system is fair.

A chunk of time is usually 30 minutes of no-screen time (including phone – apart from when they need to phone for safety reasons). We then add up these chunks of time. It is really good to have a daily chart or note the time on the fridge for when the child has the screen time back. To do this your child has to normally have clear allocated technology time, so that this time frame can be incrementally taken away from. For example, if your kids normally have technology time from 9 a.m. -12 a.m. on weekends and holidays, on these days there is a three-hour window that can be broken down into 6 x 30-minute time chunks. If your child needs a consequence more than six times a day, make the time chunks fifteen minutes from the outset, so you have 12 × 15-minute chunks (you're being easier on them with the amount of tech time taken from them per chunk, but they won't know that). Alternatively, the time chunks taken away can be carried over to tomorrow's technology time. If your child tantrums about getting off technology, then this is a negative behaviour. They get an instruction 'Time to get off technology', one warning, and then the consequence of a time chunk less next time they are on technology. If they continue to be defiant then you continue these steps and they will lose more and more technology. Brilliant! It will be a powerful lesson; this deterrent works like a dream as they learn that you mean what you say.

The age that you go from Time Out to withdrawal of privileges is up to parent judgement of what works best for your individual child. But use Time Out for as long as you can.

Some rare older kids are not into technology, so what consequence do you use once they are too old for Time Out? Basically, find what their currency is. They will not want you to know what this is. Perhaps it is being allowed to visit a neighbour for a play or to hang out, or perhaps it is riding their bike. Whatever is the thing they enjoy, use it. It sounds cruel, but taking away their privileges (in a fair and measured way) is your leverage.

What age do we start Time Out? This is also a judgement call. It depends a lot on the maturity of the child. If they understand the concept and they are capable of starting to self-soothe, then it's the right age. I have seen that kids between the ages of five and six years old typically are old enough for Time Out. But it really is a parent call. Prior to this age, we do '**Time In**'.

Time In
Time In is the same concept as Time Out, in that the child is taken to a quiet space and taken away from play time. The parent then sits with the child for a few minutes and has Time In with them. The child is learning that there is a brief break in their freedom to play due to their poor behaviour choices. It is not scary at all because the parent is with them. The parent, of course, needs to remain calm and neutral in emotion. This is really to short-circuit their bad behaviour and give them a gentle consequence. Even if the young child is tantruming throughout, once a few minutes has passed you let them out of Time In. They are too young to self-soothe, so this is not our goal. When they misbehave again, we just go straight back to the Time In. The same rule of first giving a warning applies (except for behaviour involving harm to others or objects). This Time In sets the child up to understand the concept of Time Out when they get older – which, hopefully, if you have got them on track from the outset, you rarely have to use.

Following through
If you have asked your child to do something and they have

not, then after Time Out, or after you have taken away a technology chunk of time, you bring them straight back to the original request. If they are older, this would be once you have told them that they have lost their chunk of technology. So, 'Carlo, you need to come back and make your bed.' Or, 'Emma, you have just lost a chunk of technology time, so we are going to try again. I need to you to come and put your clothes away.' This cycle then repeats and repeats. Their defiance is hurting them, not you. They will decide to get on board.

It is important to keep in mind that once you have this set up and it's your family routine, you will most likely find that you don't need to use it very much. You have done the hard work of enforcing the consequences and they have worked as a deterrent. The kids make better choices, and parents don't need to respond with the consequences. You have all earnt this improved peace in the home.

Time Out ruined
Just a note: Time Out is absolutely ruined by parents doing it upside down and inside out. When done with low awareness it can actually make the behaviour worse because it can involve giving the children your time and emotion.

How parents get it wrong is by getting really upset and giving the child lots of emotion before and during Time Out, and by lecturing the child and engaging with the child before and during Time Out. The parent is yelling at the child while putting their kids into Time Out, and yelling back to them during Time Out. What a disaster. And how incredibly common it is to get this wrong.

Also, parents in their exasperation make massive consequences for a behaviour, like a month with no technology, or clearing the child's room of all toys. What is this going to do? It is going to show that you are desperate, so, ironically, you are going to look vulnerable to the child's subconscious mind. You are also going to seem unfair, so they will resent you. The child will feel despondent, hopeless and helpless. You are going to induce a depressed state in your child. A depressed child is not going to care; they are going to throw their hands up in the air, thinking *Why bother? I may as well misbehave a lot; it's all out of my control anyway*. You have engineered a child who is going to escalate.

TEENAGERS AND CHORES – TIMING

With up to middle-school-aged children (around age thirteen), it is reasonable to expect they will do a chore or behaviour that you have asked them to do (like cleaning their teeth) straight away. They are not going to do a good job of holding that chore in their mind and finishing what they are doing first. So, getting them to 'jump to it' now is fair and required.

But teenagers need a half-hour rule. You are showing them respect by recognising that they can organise their time and that what they are doing is important to them. But the half-hour rule means respect to you also, in that what you have asked of them needs to become their priority. So ask, for example, 'Tom, can you put the washing out in the next half hour?', then set an alarm (my oven timer is going to die from overuse one day) for half an hour, and then follow it up. If they have not done it in that half hour, then you ask them to do it now. It is really a great idea to explain the format to them beforehand. Get everyone on board. If they don't get in and do the job straight away, then you give them the warning that if they don't in the next five minutes, they will lose technology time. You are calm and bored in your tone. They do the job, great; you may spin the wheel and this might be one of the times that you positively reinforce them (yes, teenagers still need appreciation and positive parent fuelling; you just do it in an age-appropriate way – you suggest going for a walk, or a coffee or milkshake). If they don't get in and do this job, then you take a technology chunk of time from them (which has been pre-arranged and is therefore a fair deterrent).

All of these specialised parenting skills are essential so that we create a cause-and-effect environment whereby it becomes our tricky (positively oriented) kids' priority to behave well. We are working to shape their internal motivation. Everyone wins: the children are getting their parent's emotion and time through positive means and the parent is able to enjoy their child and teenager because their parenting is bringing out the best in them.

CHAPTER 14
NEVER, NEVER, *NEVER* SAY SOMETHING THAT YOU CANNOT CARRY THROUGH ON AND CONTROL

This advice is in the 'speak before you think' category. We often threaten a consequence that we cannot or do not want to follow through on. When this happens, we leave ourselves very exposed to the teenager or child no longer believing what we say and losing respect for us. Our words should be gold and used cautiously and sparingly. Our children need to know that we mean what we say, and that we follow through.

It is important that you do not say something you cannot carry through on because it is beyond your control, like 'If you don't clean up your room, then your friend Lola can't come over,' when in fact you are locked in to mind Lola. Or 'If you keep hitting your brother, you won't go to the soccer final.' When in truth you fully intend to take him to play in this game.

Just slow it down and think. These actions that we can't control and don't follow through with are all punishments, not deterrents, so it's best not to be pulling these out of your hat anyway. There is a danger of setting yourself up to lose potency in what you say if you do not intend or have the capacity to follow through. Remember: your words are gold; calm yourself, take it slow, use planned deterrents.

CHAPTER 15
TIME TOGETHER

We are always given opportunities for time together, if we only look creatively. The question is whether or not we see them. A sad sight is a parent and a child going for a walk, both of them with their earphones in. Parents complain about driving their kids around, when this is potentially positive time with their child. During grocery shopping, you and your child could be working out their school subject selection. During time spent cooking, or time spent doing yard work together, the parent and child could chat about the dramas with school friends.

These are the windows in which the child does not feel pressured, and they are more likely to talk about their life events as they happen. Time is not given to us on a platter; we need to *find* time every day for our family members. Also, whenever you have a window in which to have a meaningful relationship connection, take it – take it with both hands.

Whenever an 'I love you' or an 'I'm sorry' comes your way, stop your productive mode, and take a moment to engage with these precious moments.

CHAPTER 16
THEIR FRIENDS ARE CRUCIAL

As children get older, they start to look to their friends for a sense of inclusion, a sense of identity, and intimate conversation. They want to know that they can belong. This is very difficult when their peers are just kids who can be cruel and impulsive. It is the parent's job to be sensitive to this developmental shift towards focusing on friendship connections. We need to be mindful of our young teen's need for acceptance. I'm not saying to go out and buy all the latest things to help your teen feel part of the group; I'm saying keep the dialogue open so that you know what the group dynamics are and understand the pressures that your teenager is facing. If the friendship group is going somewhere like the movies, appreciate that it is probably important for your child to be able to go, because this builds a sense of inclusion. Golden rule: never, never, *never* embarrass your kid in public; they will not forgive you. This is true humiliation. Not the humorous kind, but the despairing kind. They do not have the strength to tolerate the negative attention and criticism that could come their way.

It is also a really strategic move to encourage your kids to have groups of friends outside of school. This gives them options. If school friends are not going so well, they can manage better when they have their other friends at soccer, choir, swimming, or youth group to hang out with. If all the friendship contacts are at school, and there is tension or a fallout at school, your kid can feel desperately alone and vulnerable. Best not to have all their eggs in one basket when kids and teens are so inclined to break these eggs every now and then.

CHAPTER 17
TEENS NEED TO FEEL LISTENED TO

The teenagers' private world is a very hidden place. If they open up to you it is a golden moment. Put down what you are doing, show that you are listening, and be slow to speak. Just listen. Use your best, active listening skills. Ask questions to get them to elaborate, paraphrase so that they realise you are interested and listening. Show your respect for their opinion. If and when you disagree, think: do you need to voice your disagreement? If you feel you want to, do so without discouraging them. *Remain respectful of their opinion*. Teens are eager to feel and say that parents do not understand them. It is their theme song. Do not give them ammunition for these statements, but challenge them with your beautiful listening.

The teenage years are such a precious time as teenagers are busy preparing to become their own adults. To do this they need to separate more from the parents. They need to move away from the parents and look to their own future nests and their own future flight paths. Therefore they are inclined to find a negative and a disconnection from the parents to justify this moving away. What we are working towards instead is providing gentle support and respecting their movement away from us.

CHAPTER 18
DON'T COMPARE KIDS

Limit how much you talk about your other kids in front of your child. Be very careful when and how you do bring up your other kids in conversation. We might not notice, but patterns of praising one of our kids often can easily form. The others will notice and feel in the shadow of their sibling. Sibling jealousy is a terrible thing, as it can make siblings opponents to each other.

CHAPTER 19
KIDS WHO SAY THEY ARE FAT

I have six-year-old clients who think they 'look fat'. There is something very wrong with our society for this to be becoming commonplace. Concerned parents are bringing them in. These young children are growing up constantly hearing how 'gorgeous' they look; they get dressed up like dolls and praised. This is how they have learnt to get attention and to hear that they are special and valued. They learn to listen for these words of praise from others to know that they are okay. Their self-worth is in other people's hands from this young, young age. They hear language that compares them to adult standards of attraction, like 'Look how skinny her legs are in those shorts; she looks like a teenager'. I actually heard that one today. Their relatives talk about their own bodies, clothing, exercise concerns, and their fad diets, with the children in earshot, absorbing these messages of what is important and what to fear. The adults around them model the idea that you need to look ready for sexual attention to go out. And this is all before they have watched social media, music clips and movies.

Then there are the early teenagers who are going down the rabbit hole of eating disorders and messed-up body image issues. They hate their bodies; their monkey mind is full of horrible self-loathing self-talk. These teenagers may have travelled well as children (or not), but now with the teen image focus and bombardment from social media and so on, they have begun to subscribe to the need for perfection and the need to have another person's body. They can't embrace their individuality or the miracle that is their body.

For the parents, the question is *what to do?* The answer is layered:

1. Don't engage in or allow communication about looks, image, body shape. This blanket rule needs to be shared with friends and family. Parents then need to ensure that other adults keep to this standard. This is about reprogramming our child or teenager's value system from image to character strengths. When our child says, 'How do I look?', it is a good idea to use one broad word such as 'beautiful' or 'handsome', but then to follow this up with '... but that is not what matters; it is your heart that matters, your company, your fun.' We need our kids to not get much attention for how they look. They need to be redirected to focus on their personal attributes – attributes that have substance.

2. Do not have clothes in the house that you think are a bad idea for their value system. Throw away and

do not buy overtly sexual clothing that has young girls dressing up as if they are adults. We do not want our children and teenagers in adult worlds, so why would we dress them that way? It makes no difference whether they want to buy these, or if they are given these clothes. Don't agree to buy them or have them in the house. With boys, we want them to have self-respect and to treat others with respect, so don't buy clothes for them that would make them look intimidating to someone on the street.

3. Parenting is not about being popular; it is about guiding our child and teenager to be the best version of themselves so that they can reap the reward, and in time truly feel confident.

4. Encourage them to eat healthy food quite simply by making it the only food available in the house. Farmhouse food. If you don't want your child or teen eating bad food, don't buy it. Don't facilitate contact with this food in the first place. Treats are just that: treats. You have them on the rare occasion or for events.

5. Healthy exercise is not about being regimental during these young developmental ages; it is about being active for a purpose. Encourage them to go outside and in the sun, just for the stretch, the play and the sunlight. Set it up so that they train (and exercise) as part of a sports team and in preparation for games.

This makes exercise not about their bodies, but about health and physical skill and capacity.

6. With your own exercise, don't let your children and teens know if it is linked to your self-worth. Don't speak of 'needing' to go as if you're being driven by a fear of something (like being unattractive). Share your *enjoyment* – that's it.

We set our children up for a value system that says either 'you are your own person', or 'you are a product for others to approve of or not'. Are you reinforcing that your child is valued for their substance or their wrapping?

CHAPTER 20
FAMILY AND SIBLING CULTURE OF LOVE

What family culture do you want? It is *not* inevitable that siblings will be in conflict. So many parents have said to me that it is the nature of siblings to fight, to be at war with one another. This is not true. This is just evidence that the parents themselves have this standard of behaviour as their norm. In line with the parenting approach described above, anytime someone does any harm to another, we jump in and parent. Tone of voice and language used in the household are extremely powerful. We need to set the bar high. If our kids are not speaking in a mindful, considerate and loving way towards each other, then it is not okay.

Your children need to be each other's absolute supports in life. They need to be on the same team, not opposing teams. Yes, there will be a bit of jostling for who knows the most about things, or they will compete with their athleticism. All good and natural. But verbal put-downs and slurs are a different thing – they are damaging. Your children deserve to live in a home that builds them up, rather than tears them down.

You, of course, are a key role model here. As discussed earlier, you cannot be a hypocrite and want your children to be better behaved and more mindful than you. You are the leader in the family, so set the example.

CHAPTER 21
CHANGING GEARS: PARENTING TEENAGERS

Part of parenting teenagers is providing gentle guidance. You need to be their sounding board, as they bounce ideas around – ideas like where and when they might get a casual job and what type of job, what to do with a friendship problem, and what career area to contemplate. It is important not to be too directive, but facilitate the active brainstorm of your child's interests. As parents we can create ways to trial future work avenues, for example. Perhaps set up extra work experiences and help them meet people. How are our kids and teens supposed to know what they want to do when their exposure to the world has been so limited? They are making decisions with minimal life experience. You can use *your* life experience to gently guide them. But their decision needs to be their own, as it is their life, and their unique formula for contentment.

With teenagers, the parent role changes to that of a mentor. To play this role, you have to have a solid relationship that has taught them to respect you and admire you. If you don't, why would they look to you for guidance?

You do not have this mentoring role just by being their parent, because it is *relationship* based, not power based. Teenagers really hold us to account. They hold up a mirror and let us know whether we are their 'go to' person or not. As they grow, there is a shifting of power towards more equality. Many parents don't like this. It can be confronting, but it should be celebrated as teenagers are stretching their wings into adulthood.

CHAPTER 22
FLOW IN THE FAMILY

Family life can be turned into a **flow** activity. Flow, as I have explained in more depth in other books in this series, is a state of being absorbed in and energised by a meaningful activity. If we don't work out how to make family life a flow activity, it can become boring. Relationships can become stagnant if they are not enriched through growth experiences together. To have a state of flow, we need to engage in the 'now', and in mid-term and long-term activities together. Things we can do now are meaningful activities as a family – things that challenge and reward us. This could be going for a bush walk, having a family game of tennis, or building a worm farm together.

Mid-term and long-term goals are about having something that we as a family are working towards, a common goal. It could be a camping trip, which has the family checking on the gear and brainstorming, debating and preparing for the menu. It could be further-off family travels that take research and planning. Throughout this process of working towards the goals, we are appreciating each person's unique opinions, skills, traits and individual aims. Each family member is their own individual, and as a family we need to be integrated as we work together and affect each other. There is value in the group goal, and how each person experiences that goal is important.

Having goals together is about the family having time together. It is important that the goals reflect the interests of the family members. If Mum and Dad are interested in golf and the kids are not, there is nothing to be gained by dragging the family to golf. But if all bar one of the family members enjoys hiking, but this family member enjoys photography, then we can link the interests and make sure that the photography is a major component of the planning. We can expand our interests through family time, and we need to be creative to encompass everyone's needs.

CHAPTER 23
TECHNOLOGY = KID IN A CANDY STORE; RESTRICT THE CANDY

So many parents have said to me, 'My kid won't get off technology.' They are surprised by this and disappointed and angry. Their reaction always astonishes me. I respond, 'Why would they get off? They're having fun.'

If a kid went into a candy store, we would not expect them to say, 'Okay, I'll stop now; I've had enough. I'd better be sensible.' No way; the kid would go for it. We are all Augustus Gloop (from *Charlie and the Chocolate Factory*) as kids, and this is exactly the case with technology.

> Kids do not regulate their own technology; this is 100% the parent's responsibility.

Technology is only our enemy if it is not kept in check. Your job is to work out a healthy balance for technology, and then *parent*. Take responsibility for guiding your kids and teens. This means creating the guidelines and following through, using the information outlined in this book to give you the backing. Use consequences. If your child of ten years or older doesn't get off technology when it is the right time, or they get on when it is not pre-negotiated, then they lose a chunk of the next lot of technology time. Technology is a treat; it is not a lifestyle.

If kids live on technology, they forget how to do other things: how to amuse themselves, how to enjoy a good book, how to interact, how to be human. It is sad; their childhood is lost to technology as they are not present and engaged in the world. They enter a time warp and their childhood disappears into the black hole of technology.

What amount is the right amount of technology? It is up to you. Some guidelines perhaps? No gaming during the school week, Monday to Thursday. Screen time only after homework or a certain hour is reached (7 p.m.?), so that they have time to remember how to entertain themselves. No phones or technology in bedrooms one hour before sleep time, so they can wind down and reduce their stimulation (read below). Friday night they might enjoy gaming, and Saturday and Sunday (and school holidays) no screen time between 12 and 7 p.m. Maybe they can do a bit of gaming before midday and after 7 p.m. This is only an idea; as parents you work out what you think is healthy. This is the routine that we have in my house and it works well for our big boys. Our two little ones (seven and nine) just get on their iPad for a little while when they ask, and then we get them off after not too long. We don't let them have long bouts on technology.

CHAPTER 24
SLEEP PLEASE

If your child or teenager is having trouble falling asleep or returning to sleep when they wake, have a look at Book 2, Chapter 27. The techniques work equally well for kids, with the parents taking the lead in guiding and supporting them.

YOUNG KIDS

People often talk about having trouble getting their kids to sleep in their own beds. The children either determinedly start in their parents' bed, or during the night they end up there. This seriously gets in the way of the adult having solid, undisturbed sleep, let alone adult time in their own bed. The kids also not only miss out on sound sleep, which is important for their next day's mood, behaviour and ability to learn, but they don't learn the independence of sleeping in their own beds.

I have well and truly noted that this challenge is usually with the youngest child or the only child. Almost always. Why is that? Usually it is because the older children had to move to their own bed because the next baby was coming along. The parents were forced to parent and firmly encourage their child to move to their own bed. With the youngest child, we don't have the next baby there to make us parent. We need to *decide* to be directive and firm. In my experience, the parents are not firm enough in insisting that their kids have to sleep in their own beds. The parent is either just taking the easy option and leaving things as they are, or the child knows the parent will cave in, so they emotionally pressure the parent.

I would suggest that we need an absolutely firm resolve. First, be firm with your child and try to get them to believe you, which will be hard if they have a history of having it over you. Secondly, I know this sounds strange, but treat it as a misbehaviour. If they come into your room, then they go to Time Out. Yes, this is horrible in the middle of the night. But we need the child to think, *If I go into Mum and Dad's bed, I'm not going to be able to stay there and I will just end up in Time Out, so I'd rather just stay here, in my bed*. This is calm psychological warfare; you have to create the situation so that they are motivated to stay in bed. You can do it!

TEENS

Sleep issues often stem from technology. Many, many kids are on technology into the night. They don't sleep because they are plugged in online. Some have learnt the bad habit of 'needing' technology to go to sleep. They have their phones in their rooms, so they are 'dinging' all night, available to each other 24/7. Then they present to the psychology clinic irritable and exhausted. No surprise. Again, this is the parent's job to take charge and not to assume the child or teen has any wisdom here. They are just reacting to impulsive gratification. Why wouldn't they?

Don't forget kids aged six to twelve need nine to twelve hours of quality sleep. Teens need a good eight to ten hours' sleep. Without this sleep their physical health, immune system and mental health can be adversely affected. They will have low energy, low motivation, and poor capacity to concentrate and learn. They will even become impaired in their capacity to store information in their long-term memories. Grades will go down and general behaviour all round will deteriorate. Sleep is in, and technology at night-time is out, and parents need to actively police this. When they have left school and you have instilled good habits regarding technology and sleeping, then you can hand these decisions over to them.

So, set a suitable bedtime. One hour before this time, ALL technology comes to the kitchen bench in a designated container. Just tolerate the tantrums and desperate explanations for why they need the technology. If they need the alarm on their phones, get them a separate alarm; go old school. If schoolwork needs to be done with a crammed assignment or exam preparation, then let them stay up on these rare occasions, working on the kitchen table with the screen facing you. This will deter them from the mind-numbing distraction of flicking through YouTube, Netflix and social media. When they say they need the noise to go to sleep, well that is a terrible habit to continue into the future. Time to break it. Night in, night out, persevere with tough love. They'll get tired and bored and they will learn to go to sleep un-assisted eventually. You are doing them a massive disservice letting them continue with technology-dependent sleep.

> Having a bad habit is no excuse for continuing it.

We have negotiated the tough terrain of child psychology and the rewarding yet challenging skills of parenting. Now we can turn to how to be informed parents across a range of life situations that could well come your way. To parent with confidence is such a wonderful experience. Let's help build your confidence further.

CHAPTER 25
KIDS THRIVING THROUGH PARENTAL SEPARATION

You can separate well. You can nourish your child through separation, so they are minimally affected. You just have to 'adult' really well in this situation.

Your child's sense of who they are is that they are half Mum and half Dad. So when Mum attacks Dad or Dad attacks Mum post-separation, they are attacking a massive part of the child's sense of themselves. The child feels splintered and torn. This is on top of the heartache of seeing someone you love attacking someone else that you love. It is horrible to be in the middle of this contempt. Contempt is a very strong emotion; it is this most dangerous emotion that erodes relationships and remains post-separation. Consider this a very strong warning never to show your child the contempt you feel for your ex-partner. Remain respectful towards your ex in front of your child, for the child's sake. Your child must know that you value their relationship with the other parent. Then your child can breathe out.

When a parent leaves an unhealthy marriage or de facto relationship, post-separation they have an opportunity to consolidate, recover and launch into their future. If the parent bounds ahead and becomes much healthier and happier, then the child benefits enormously. It is much better for the child to have healthy parents who are separated than to have two parents who are unhealthy because they are together. The emotional tone of the parent and the parental home shapes the child's day-to-day life. Ask yourself, which home environment is happier and healthier for the child: parents together pre-separation or the home post-separation? Provided that you are creating this calmer, more joyful home environment, then your child will thrive post-separation. Many parents feel guilty about separating. They seem to miss the point of the improved quality of day-to-day life that the child has been able to experience as well as the parent.

So many kids and teenagers have said to me, 'I wish my parents would hurry up and separate. They can't stand each other; it's horrible'. Meanwhile the parents feel guilty for separating and believe they should stay together for the kids' sake. Or maybe they know that they should separate but they are having trouble finding the courage, and citing the sake of children is a good excuse to try to justify their inaction. It really is a paradox. It is true that young children want to stick to the family concept of having Mum and Dad together, and it can be difficult for them to adjust. But provided the parents manage the separation with a positive tone, then the child will adjust.

Logistically, it is annoying going between two houses – this cannot be denied. Younger children take it in their stride, as they know no different. Setting the kids up so that they have all that they need at both houses is key. You do not want suitcase kids who have to lug the bulk of their possessions week by week. This is not fair. Set each household up as if it could run independently, and the child will then be able to breeze in and out without the material hardship.

When explaining the separation, don't bring in the adult seriousness and adult emotion. Together explain that Mum and Dad are not healthy and happy together and they need to separate to get healthy and happy. That it is sad, and it is change, but we will be okay. With time, everything will settle. They will want to know concrete details: where will they live? What bedroom? What bedspread will they have? What about the pets? Kids are concrete and they need to comprehend what this new world looks like for them. With little people you can promote the idea that they are going to have two houses not one, and two lots of birthdays and Christmases and so on. Teenagers will probably want a more complex explanation, but try to stay away from adult disclosure. You don't want them to get caught up in the conflict that would complicate their relationship with the other parent, or rush what is left of their childhood into the world of adult pressures.

CHAPTER 26
TEENS BECOME CAVE DWELLERS

A quick note: you know your child has morphed into an early teenager when they start to isolate themselves in their room. They cocoon themselves in their room. Please know this is normal. It is not a personal affront to you; they are not being rude; they are not rejecting you. They are doing what comes naturally. They are becoming much more interested in their own world than in the family. They are also needing to separate a little from the family, and are moving more towards being influenced by their friends. They are starting to try to work out how to be their own person, with their own personal world and their own friendship networks.

Be patient. Don't go in and pester them often. Insist on dinner at the table always. No phones on the table. And insist that they come out with the family once per weekend if you can manage it. They will probably be reluctant, but you insist. Tailor the outing to their needs and once you have them out of the house, they are perhaps likely to engage with the family more. Or not? They will keep their earphones in, listening to music. That is okay for the road trip, but the moment there are people together, insist that there are no earphones in, as this is socially rude and isolating. You are teaching them manners regarding technology and social interaction. If you are not popular with this, you are doing a good job parenting.

CHAPTER 27
MONEY MANAGEMENT SKILLS

Do you want your child to feel that as a family member they are responsible for contributing to the household? To pitch in with their share? Yes? Good, then don't pay them with pocket money for routine home chores. If you pay them, it is as if they are doing you a favour. And they can simply say, 'No, I don't want the money, I won't do the job.' What are you going to say? You have just set that up.

Kids do jobs because you have asked them to and they are a contributing part of the family. Full stop. It is good for them to have their assigned jobs that perhaps don't rotate around, so that they have a sense of routine and ownership, and there is less constant negotiation. But money education is also very important. I am a big fan of pocket money coming weekly. Perhaps $1 per year of age per week. So a seven-year-old gets $7 per week, and a ten-year-old gets $10 per week. But here is the clincher: this money is for everything that they want throughout the year. All the fun stuff. Not clothes (unless the clothes are for fun). And pocket money is not to be used for junk food.

What this means is that your child learns that when you go to a shop, and they ask to buy something, your response is, 'Well, that depends; how much money have you got – and are you sure that that is what you want to spend your money on?' The child learns that if they impulsively spend their money, their money is gone. They experience the regret of having no money left over, and they have to forgo the big-ticket items. Most kids begin to value money because it is *their* money. They absolutely stop asking their parents for things because the responsibility gets put back onto them. Also, they usually learn to save up their money because they can, and they feel empowered. They figure out that delayed gratification means that they can work towards bigger items that are truly rewarding to them. Or maybe they just learn to enjoy saving money.

You can pay your kids for big jobs, but again, I think you should be very careful in doing this. We want our kids to learn to help out because that is just what they do, not on the condition of getting money. Perhaps if they do something that involves a huge amount of labour, like laying lawn at Grandma's house for the day, then we pay them. But I would not pay kids for helping clean the family car or cleaning up the backyard.

CHAPTER 28
SIGNIFICANT CLINICAL CONDITIONS: IF IN DOUBT, GET HELP

Obsessive compulsive disorder, depression, anxiety, eating disorder behaviours, body image problems, low self-esteem, bullying, gender identity issues, extreme defiant behaviour, phobias, self-harm, sleep problems, trauma, adjustment difficulties, separation anxiety. These are just a few of a long list of very real problems that children and teenagers face, and they do not usually just 'sort themselves out'. They actually have a tendency to get worse and can set into lifelong struggles. So please, if in doubt, get help; see a clinical psychologist who specialises with children and nip the problems in the bud. Let them move on with their childhood and teenagehood without these clinical problems casting a dark shadow over their precious youth. Psychology is about getting in, sorting it out, and then leaving you to enjoy the rewards from becoming healthy.

CHAPTER 29
SCHOOL IS LIKE A ZOO

I was on a cruise ship, and a girl aged perhaps twelve was sitting next to me at a communal table. She randomly started to tell me that she found school really hard. In her experience, kids were sometimes kind, but sometimes mean. There were the kids who stirred all the time, who made up rumours and spread them for entertainment and drama. Then there were the friendship groups that changed with the mood of the group. She could not keep up, and she felt exhausted and apprehensive. How we got onto the topic I do not know.

My fairly automatic response, just like in a session, was that 'this is all true'. I asked the girl how she would describe school broadly. What is it like? Are the kids sensible? 'No,' she said with a smile. Her mother was listening intently, knowing I was a child psychologist and hoping to get a freebie to help her parent. So I asked, 'Does it seem like a zoo?' Each of the different kids and groups of kids are like different animals. Some just want to goof around and throw jokes at you; they are like annoying monkeys. Some cannot be trusted; they are like snakes. Some are all about drama; they are the hyenas. Some are very changeable, and they are cats: your friend until they are not.

I explained to this girl, who hung on my every word, that there are some puppy dogs just like herself. Who are kind and consistent, want to have a good time and do no harm. The other kids have got some growing up to do. They are not puppy dogs yet, but most of them will be. So school is about having to be patient with all of the chaos that the social world of kids creates, working out who is who, anticipating their difficult behaviour and being on the front foot in coping. Sidestep them, realise their behaviour is about them trying to meet their needs or deal with insecurities, not about you. Dramas will come and go, so hold your breath; you will swim through it and come out the other side and then it will be some other poor child's turn.

In the adult world we would call this profiling, but with children, 'animals in a zoo' works well. The schoolyard is legitimately a tough gig, but our kids have to get through their tricky school environment. Having their eyes open to what they are dealing with and learning not to personalise tricky people is an amazing life skill that serves children well early in life. It is wonderful to share this wisdom with them as you are their support crew while they wrestle through school crises. When they come home from school, ask them, 'How was the zoo today?'

CHAPTER 30
TEENAGERS WHO VOTE US OUT

Children automatically put their parents on a pedestal. There is no qualification process; you are just put there by default. This is because the child needs to think well of you to feel secure in their world. A large part of their self-concept comes from their link with and their internalising of their parent/s, so if they think well of their parent, they can think well of themselves. 'You're okay so I'm okay'. They also don't have critical analysis fine-tuned yet.

Teenagers, however, are a completely different ball game. They decide if you deserve to be on a pedestal and where exactly you sit in their esteem. You do need to earn the respect of your teenager. It is ridiculous to demand respect from a teenager. Yes, you can require them to behave respectfully towards yourself and others, absolutely. But actually *having* respect for you is a different matter. The teenager looks to you to assess whether you are fair and emotionally safe for them, and whether you live according to your espoused values and to solid values. A teenager sniffs out hypocrisy and will not tolerate it.

Teenagers are becoming independent thinkers; they are busy working out their own selves, their own values, their own flight paths, their people and their future nests. And you're either a solid asset, or you are disappointing to them. They can love you, but not admire you. This is a horrible truth. I have spent thousands of hours talking very personally with teenagers, and I can tell you, this is absolutely their reality. It is during the early teenage years, thirteen to fourteen, that accountability really starts to kick in, and from there it continues.

If a parent has been a bully, neglectful, abusive and/or manipulative, the teenager, provided that they are not beaten down into submission, will toss this parent from their world. They will distance themselves and disconnect. It is this age that some parents lose touch with their children. It is very sad but not at all surprising. Many dominant and abusive parents seem to think that their children will remain children forever and that they can just continue to take advantage of the power difference. They see the child as a possession, a right. They really miss the reality that the child grows up and has their own voice and their own vote. This 'power over the child' mindset is very short-sighted behaviour, but it is consistent with this impulsive and mindless type of parenting profile.

IN CONCLUSION

Our primary goal of parenting is to have our children feel cherished, loved and safe. We want to instil in them a sense that it is possible to be happy in our uncertain world. This means instilling the crucial ingredients of hope and belief in themselves, others and their future – the antidote to depression and anxiety. It is our *actions* that role model this life attitude, not our words. If we want them to feel determined and self-believing, then we cannot parent them with criticism and lecturing. We cannot bully them into behaving. Given love and support, most children grow into happy, productive adults.

Doing a good job of parenting requires us to be the best version of ourselves. This is their gift to us.

The horizon that must guide us in our parenting is the question of what kind of adults do we want to grow, and have we behaved in a way that will earn their respect and admiration when they too join us in the adult world. Accountability is key to approaching parenting with a proactive and intentional mindset.

Many of us have dreamt of having children, or indeed assumed we would reach this milestone in life. And then we discover that the road is as challenging as it is rewarding.

Know that you are not alone. When clients present in session and rank their most significant stressors in their life, inevitably it is their parenting or relationship with their children and their ongoing fears for their children (young or adult) that rates pretty high. While we are not given a manual for raising children when they come into our care, hopefully this book is the next best thing. Good on you for taking the time to read this. If you apply half of these lessons you will be miles ahead. Most of us limp along in the murky waters of how to parent. You have just reached for some pretty effective oars.

FURTHER READING

If you wish to learn more about 'understanding your humanness', you might like to try the other books in the 'Signposts for Living' series by Dr Kirsten Hunter:

Book 1: Control your Consciousness – In the Driver's Seat

Book 2: Understanding Myself – Be an Expert

Book 3: Mindfulness and State of Flow – Living with Purpose and Passion

Book 4: Understanding Others – Loved Ones to Tricky Ones

Book 6: Nailing Being an Adult – Have the Skills

ACKNOWLEDGEMENTS

To Jon, my beautiful husband, your support is constant. I can always rely on you to be in my corner, patiently championing me on while I sit typing away. With writing, having someone who believes in you makes all the difference. Thank you that it is always 'us' facing the next challenge, the next hurdle. I love you.

My devoted mum has been the rock through my childhood and every chapter of my adulthood. No child could have a more extraordinary mum. I'm proud of you and I love you.

Our five boys, Lachlan, James, Tobias, Jack, and George, when you heard that your mum was writing books, non-fiction and fiction, your response was simply 'of course she is'. When you heard mum was publishing, your response was 'of course she is'. When we talk about the book being successful in reaching a wide audience, your response, 'of course it will'. You boys are so beautiful. Ever-resounding support, thank you. I love you.

Vanya Lowther, you are the smartest person I know, and perhaps the wisest. You are also my closest and my lifelong friend. Thank you for taking on the mammoth task of being the first person to put your eyes on the *Signposts for Living* books. Your perseverance, your contribution and brainpower was and is so appreciated. I love you.

Jane Smith, I agree with Stephen King, 'to write is human, to edit is divine'. Thank you for your eye for detail, your grammatical wizardry and staying fresh when there was so much work to do. You're a talented gem.

ABOUT THE AUTHOR

Dr Kirsten Hunter is a clinical psychologist with 20 years' experience working with children, adolescents, adults, and couples across the expanse of clinical areas. Between running her private practice, enjoying time with her family, and writing her books, Kirsten juggles a range of passions – particularly for scuba diving and hiking. Kirsten is known for diving deep into life, creating and embracing all of life's opportunities. Born in Brisbane, she now lives in Toowoomba, Australia, with her six men: her husband and their five sons. Even their pets are male ...

www.ingramcontent.com/pod-product-compliance
Lightning Source LLC
Chambersburg PA
CBHW041958080526
44588CB00021B/2790